Off with her head!

Anne Boleyn was young and flirty – and Henry fell madly in love with her. But after they had been married for three years and Anne had still failed to give Henry a son, he got angry. Anne was accused of being unfaithful. Henry had her arrested and sent for trial at the Tower of London. She was found guilty and executed two days later.

I'll never get out of here alive!

Two weeks later, Henry married Jane Seymour. She did have a son, Edward, who became king after Henry died.

After Anne was executed, baby Elizabeth went to live with her half-sister Mary who was 17 years older.

Anne Boleyn arrived as a prisoner at Traitor's Gate. She was beheaded with a sword on Tower Green

Keeping my head

'Growing up was a tricky time for me. My father had six wives before I was ten! I never knew how they would treat me. But my governess, Kat Ashley, helped a lot.'

Henry said that his first two wives and children didn't count. Nevertheless, Henry made sure Elizabeth was well educated.

Henry's sixth wife, Katherine Parr, was kind to all Henry's children. She helped Henry to become closer to Mary and Elizabeth. He agreed that if Edward died, they would reign in turn.

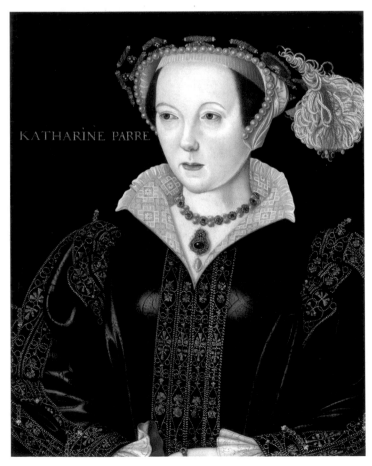

KATHARINE PARRE

Elizabeth's last step-mother, Katherine Parr

When Henry died in 1547, his Protestant son Edward became king. Katherine Parr married Thomas Seymour but she died a year later.

What about Thomas Seymour's plans to marry Princess Elizabeth?

A close shave!

When Katherine Parr died, Thomas Seymour thought he would make a good husband for the 15-year-old Elizabeth. Unfortunately, Thomas also made secret plans to control Edward, now king. Thomas was arrested and executed for treason!

Then Elizabeth, Kat and her servants were interrogated about her plans to marry Thomas. Nobody could prove anything, so they survived – just!

THOMAS LORD SEYMOUR

Thomas Seymour

Err... I vaguely remember talking about it...

Well, we certainly weren't planning a secret wedding.

Umm... I sort of knew that Thomas Seymour had his eye on Elizabeth...

They're lying but I can't prove it. Drat!

Then danger struck again! When Mary became queen, she re-introduced the Catholic religion. She thought Elizabeth, a Protestant, was plotting against her. Mary had Elizabeth imprisoned in the Tower. But she kept her head – by a whisker.

God save the Queen!

Hatfield, 17 November 1558

'I became Queen on the day Mary died. I knew I could trust William Cecil, so I immediately made him privy councillor, my most important adviser.'

The day before her coronation, Elizabeth left the Tower of London for Westminster Abbey to be crowned. It had been snowing and there was deep mud on the ground. Every so often, Elizabeth stopped to talk to people or to watch entertainment like the Spanish acrobat who slid down a rope attached to St Paul's steeple.

Elizabeth was crowned on 15 January 1559. She was 25 years old. Every year celebrations were held and bells rang out to mark the day she became Queen.

It's one of the best days ever! Hundreds of people are lining the route. The Queen looks fantastic. She's being carried on a special seat trimmed with real gold cloth and led by beautiful white horses.

Finding a husband

'People were always trying to marry me off but when I came to the throne I was unmarried. Of course, as soon as I became Queen, all sorts of no-hopers thought they'd try their luck.'

Kings, archdukes and assorted princes were all turned down. King Erik of Sweden was even refused because he wasn't fashionable enough. However, Elizabeth became very friendly with Robert Dudley, Earl of Leicester, but he was already married.

One day, Leicester's wife, Amy Robsart, was found dead with a broken neck at the bottom of some stairs.

Dearest, loveliest Elizabeth,
You will have heard that Amy has been found dead. I know that people are saying that I had her murdered! But I didn't! Honest! I do hope that when all the gossip has died down you will agree to marry me.
Your ever loving Leicester

Unfortunately, Elizabeth couldn't risk marrying a suspected murderer.

The 'frog' prince

Later, Francis, Duke of Anjou and brother of the French king, came courting. He had a rough voice, terrible skin, a big nose and bandy legs! Elizabeth adored him and called him her 'frog'. Unfortunately, Elizabeth's advisors did not want her to marry him because he was a Catholic. Tearfully she had to say goodbye.

Francis, Duke of Anjou

Finally, when Elizabeth was an old woman she fell for Robert Devereux, Earl of Essex. When he secretly married a young widow, she banished him from court. She forgave him but when he planned a rebellion against her, Essex was arrested and executed.

The old Queen was very sad that Essex betrayed her. She became very depressed after his death and was never quite the same again.

Help! I'm in love with someone else!

Robert Devereux, Earl of Essex

9

My favourite palace

Greenwich Palace

'I loved Greenwich. Once, we had a mock battle with Leicester on one side and an admiral on the other. The two sides pretended to battle it out. Afterwards everybody cheered me and I cheered back.'

> This armour cost a fortune!

Greenwich was Elizabeth's favourite palace outside London. Here, she welcomed the best musicians, poets and entertainers. Elizabeth was especially fond of tilts in which two knights on horseback tried to break each other's lances.

This tilting armour belonged to the Earl of Leicester

Elizabeth was an excellent musician. This orpharion (a type of lute) belonged to her

Elizabeth loved to receive bags of sweets

At New Year everyone gave presents. Gifts depended on who you were. Nobles and bishops gave the Queen gold, jewels and expensive clothes. Servants gave luxury foods such as ginger and marzipan or bags filled with sweetmeats.

Elizabeth also gave gifts, mostly money. The more important you were, the more money you got.

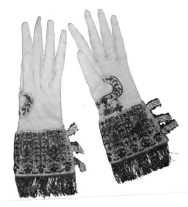

These gloves were a gift to Elizabeth when she visited Oxford University. They were too big, so she left them behind

Elizabeth's court

Elizabeth was always surrounded by hundreds of nobles, advisers and servants. Everyone hoped to attract the Queen's attention. If she liked you, it could bring fame and fortune. If you angered her you could be banished from court, or even imprisoned!

What to wear?

'I was especially fond of jewels. I inherited lots from my father and others were presents. But some were stolen treasure bought back by my explorers!'

Getting dressed was a lengthy business for noblewomen. One man said it was quicker to rig a ship! After dressing, a cloth was arranged over Elizabeth's clothes and her red hair cleaned by rubbing it with a warm cloth and combing it. Then her hair was styled and sometimes false hair or a head-dress was added.

Elizabeth's leather riding boots with cork heels

Queen Elizabeth wore richly decorated gowns decorated with jewels, embroidery and lace. Her favourite colours were black and white

In Tudor times, most people had rotten teeth. When she died, Elizabeth had very few teeth left. She disguised her toothless mouth by padding it out!

This medal was made to mark Elizabeth's recovery from smallpox

Smallpox is a deadly disease and in Tudor times it killed lots of people. If they survived, it left them with horrible pock-marks. In 1562 Elizabeth nearly died of smallpox, but according to people who saw her, she had no scars at all.

Elizabeth had a keen sense of smell. She used scent in bottles like this one to disguise nasty smells!

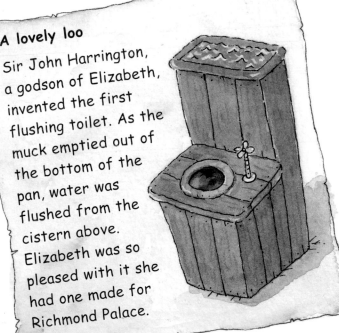

A lovely loo

Sir John Harrington, a godson of Elizabeth, invented the first flushing toilet. As the muck emptied out of the bottom of the pan, water was flushed from the cistern above. Elizabeth was so pleased with it she had one made for Richmond Palace.

Fool's gold

Greenwich, 1576

'Greenwich was the nearest royal palace to the mouth of the river Thames. I loved waving to my explorers as they sailed by on their way to new worlds.'

In the 1570s, England wanted to trade woollen cloth in Asia in exchange for silk, furs and spices. The problem was that Spain and Portugal, the most powerful seafaring nations, controlled the best routes to Asia around Africa and over the Pacific, via Central America.

So the search was on to find the fabled North-West and North-East Passages. The possible routes were either above North America or Russia. Both passages were very dangerous and frozen for most of the year.

Nutmeg was an expensive spice. People carried it around with graters like this one to put in drinks and on food.

The North-West Passage

In 1576, Martin Frobisher sailed westwards. He crossed the Atlantic and reached present-day Baffin Island. Once there, Frobisher found some black rock that he thought contained gold and silver. He was so excited he forgot all about new routes and dreamt about getting rich!

Martin Frobisher

Mid-Atlantic, 1578

We've got a cargo of black rock which is going to make me rich very soon. We've also got three captured Inuit aboard, a man called Collichang, a woman called Egnock and her son Nutiok. On our last voyage five sailors went missing – we suspected foul play. So we've taken these people as hostages. When we get back to England I'm going to show them to the Queen and then make a bit of money by putting them on display.

Egnock and her son, Nutiok in her hood

Unfortunately, the rock proved worthless. Nobles, merchants and Elizabeth herself lost money they had invested, hoping for a share of the profits. Sadly, Collichang, Egnock and Nutiok all died shortly after arriving in England.

Big ideas

'My cleverest adviser, John Dee, persuaded me that England had conquered America centuries ago – so it was really part of my empire'

Spain and Portugal controlled the trade with South America and shipped vast amounts of silver and gold back. Everyone at Elizabeth's court could see how rich those countries had become. Now they wanted some of the fabulous treasure for themselves!

Seamen used this back-staff to find their position at sea. It was invented by an Englishman, Captain John Davis

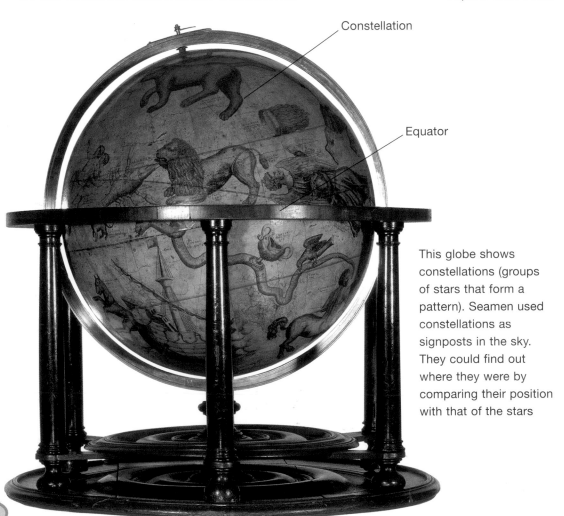

Constellation

Equator

This globe shows constellations (groups of stars that form a pattern). Seamen used constellations as signposts in the sky. They could find out where they were by comparing their position with that of the stars

At this time, Spain and Portugal had the biggest navies and best seamen. People did not believe that England was a great power. Dee told Elizabeth that if she was to beat Spain and Portugal, she needed more ships, better maps and new instruments for finding the way at sea. He saw to it that important Spanish and Portuguese sailing books were translated into English for seamen to use.

The Mariners' Mirrour was a book of charts, views of coastlines, tables and sailing directions. It was very useful for sailors

A map of the North Pole drawn by Gerard Mercator, one of the best map-makers of the time. Notice the mountain at its centre – it's totally made-up!

My special pirate

'When Francis Drake set sail from Plymouth, I knew he planned to attack Spanish ships. Of course, I pretended not to know, otherwise Spain would have declared war.'

Francis Drake's ship, the *Golden Hind*, was a merchant ship designed to carry cargo

Ha! I'm off to make trouble for the Spanish!

Francis Drake

mainmast

main sail

aftercastle

stern

rudder

keel

gunports

rigging

upper deck

forecastle

main deck

bow

cargo hold

Drake was planning to anger Spain by attacking their ports in South America. He also had his eye on the fabulous treasure being shipped back to Spain.

Drake followed routes unknown to English seamen. To help him, he carried a description of the first round-the-world voyage that had been completed fifty years earlier by Ferdinand Magellan, a Portuguese.

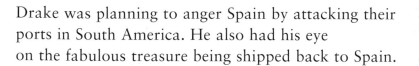

Spanish 'pieces of eight'

To whoever finds this letter

Francis Drake, that horrible English pirate, spotted my ship. He slowed his ship right down so as not to alert us. Then, as it got dark, he came alongside. He pretended to be friendly and said a few words in Spanish. Then suddenly he opened fire, crippling our ship! We were sunk!

Treasure!

During the voyage, a Spanish sailor was captured. He was tortured and forced to reveal that a Spanish ship was carrying a huge cargo of silver back to Spain. If Drake could get it back to England he would be a millionaire!

England's greatest sailor

Greenwich, 1580

'Little did I realise that when Drake set off, he'd become the first Englishman to sail round the world. What a hero!'

News of Drake's raids reached Philip II of Spain and the Spanish were out to get him. Drake had to outwit them so he decided to return by crossing the Pacific. It was a dangerous voyage, never yet completed by an Englishman. The Spanish thought he'd never make it. Then they realised that he had a captured Portuguese sea captain aboard with maps showing the best route back!

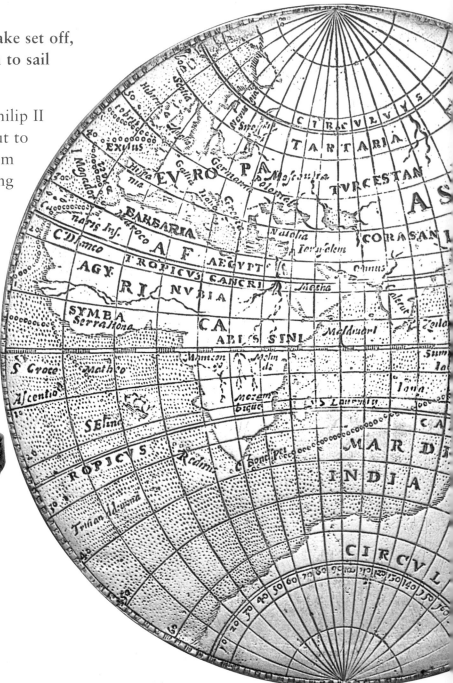

Drake stole four chests of precious Chinese porcelain from Spanish ships. This bowl may have been part of the loot

Elizabeth gave this jewel to Drake

Three years after setting off, Drake reached England becoming the first Englishman to sail round the world. Elizabeth gave a great banquet in his honour and allowed him to keep some of the Spanish loot he'd stolen. She rewarded him with a knighthood, jewels and land. He was a national hero!

This silver medal was made to honour Drake's round the world voyage. The dotted line shows the route he took.

21

Greedy eyes on America

'Drake proved that we could do just as well as Spain and Portugal. It made everyone feel confident and ready for the next challenge – settling America'.

In 1584, Walter Ralegh gathered together people who wanted to settle America. They thought that cheap land and trade would make them rich. Maybe they would discover Indian treasure too! Elizabeth agreed to the plans but said that they would have to raise the money for the voyages themselves.

Walter Ralegh

John White was a good artist who went on the voyage to America. His job was to record the native people, flowers and animals

BOLADORA.

The mystery of Roanoke

The first colony of 107 people was set up at Roanoke on the east coast of North America. It was a failure and the colonists returned to England within a year. A second colony was set up but when explorers returned there three years later, there was no sign of anyone. Had everyone died? Had Indians captured them? Had they got fed up and wandered off? The mystery is still unsolved!

Two North American Indians. The little girl holds an Elizabethan doll, given to her by an English settler

This drawing shows the Indian village of Secoton, south of Roanoke. Notice the ceremony in the bottom right hand corner

Eventually, a colony did survive. The colonists learned to farm local crops including maize and tobacco for their own use and to trade with England.

The Spanish Armada

Plymouth, 1588

'I knew that it was only a matter of time before Spain wanted revenge for all our attacks on Spanish ships and colonies. Sure enough, earlier this year my spies informed me that Spain was preparing to invade us.'

In 1588, the mighty Spanish Armada set sail for England. The plan was to sail up the English Channel, pick up an army from the Netherlands and invade England.

English ships were small, fast and carried lots of guns

Large Spanish ships could carry lots of troops but were not so easy to handle

24

Meanwhile, the English assembled 128 warships and 40 armed merchant ships, 8,350 seamen to sail the ships, 2,080 servants to work below deck, 19,290 soldiers to fight and 2,630 large guns to fire 123,790 cannon balls.

Everyone was overjoyed when the Spanish Armada was defeated. This medal was probably given to those who helped

1. English ships fired at the Armada as it sailed up the English Channel and anchored near Calais ...

2. Then the English sent fire-ships towards the Spanish ships so that they would catch alight and burn ...

3. The Spanish cut their anchor cables and fled. Several ran aground or were wrecked ...

4. The English chased the Armada up to the North Sea. Less than a third of the Spanish ships, made it back to Spain.

Spies, lies and murder!

'I lost count of the plots to murder me! Sir Francis Walsingham set up a secret service that discovered three plots to overthrow me in a single year!'

Mary had re-introduced the Catholic religion. When Elizabeth became queen, she changed the religion back to the Protestant Church of England. This made some Catholics angry and they plotted ways to get Mary, Queen of Scots, (Elizabeth's Catholic cousin), on the throne.

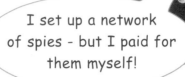

I set up a network of spies - but I paid for them myself!

Sir Francis Walsingham

Mary, Queen of Scots, had troubles too. First, one of her servants was killed with her husband's dagger. Then her husband, Lord Darnley, was found strangled. To make matters worse, Mary then married the Earl of Bothwell, who was suspected of Darnley's murder!

Elizabeth's spymaster, Sir Francis Walsingham, said that Mary, Queen of Scots was plotting to have Elizabeth killed. Her advisers wanted her to get rid of Mary. Elizabeth didn't want to sign the death warrant of a queen, but she finally agreed and Mary was executed. Other people involved in the plot were hung, drawn and quartered – the punishment for treason.

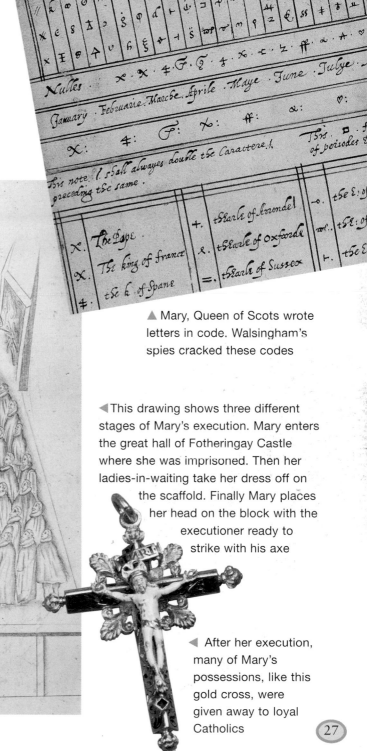

▲ Mary, Queen of Scots wrote letters in code. Walsingham's spies cracked these codes

◄ This drawing shows three different stages of Mary's execution. Mary enters the great hall of Fotheringay Castle where she was imprisoned. Then her ladies-in-waiting take her dress off on the scaffold. Finally Mary places her head on the block with the executioner ready to strike with his axe

◄ After her execution, many of Mary's possessions, like this gold cross, were given away to loyal Catholics

The Queen is dead

Richmond Palace, 1603

'As Archbishop of Canterbury, I held the old Queen's hand as she lay dying. She was 69 and had been poorly for about a fortnight.'

Elizabeth's body was taken by river barge from Richmond to Whitehall Palace, in London. Tens of thousands of people lined the route of the funeral procession to Westminster Abbey where she was buried.

When she was an old woman, Elizabeth was described as having a hooked nose and no teeth

This is the saddest day ever. I'm weeping as the funeral chariot goes past surrounded by the royal bodyguard all dressed in black. Elizabeth was the best Queen we ever had!

Elizabeth reigned for 44 years and died at a greater age than any previous king or queen. She survived plots to kill her and saw England grow in confidence to overcome powerful enemies, she witnessed some of the greatest achievements in English history. Her death marked the end of the Tudors.

God Save King James!

King James I of England and VI of Scotland

Elizabeth had no children. Earlier in her reign, it was clear that James, the Protestant son of Mary, Queen of Scots, should succeed her when she died. King James I of England and VI of Scotland became the first person to rule England and Scotland together.

Map of the world

This map shows where Elizabeth's explorers went.

Baffin Island

Greenwich

Bristol

Inuit

Plymouth

NORTH AMERICA

Roanoake

NORTH ATLANTIC OCEAN

Portugal

Spain

CENTRAL AMERICA

SOUTH AMERICA

SOUTH ATLANTIC OCEAN

PACIFIC OCEAN

A

Timeline

1533 ✪ Elizabeth is born at Greenwich Palace

1536 ✪ Anne Boleyn is beheaded

1547 ✪ Henry dies and is succeeded by his son, Edward VI

1553 ✪ Edward dies and is succeeded by Mary

1558 ✪ Mary dies and is succeeded by Elizabeth

1559 ✪ Elizabeth is crowned

1562 ✪ Elizabeth nearly dies of smallpox

1567 ✪ Darnley is murdered

1576 ✪ Martin Frobisher sets off on his first voyage to find the North-West Passage

1579 ✪ The Duke of Anjou courts Elizabeth

1580 ✪ Francis Drake becomes the first Englishman to sail round the world

1584 ✪ The first colony is set up at Roanoke, North America

1587 ✪ Mary, Queen of Scots is executed

1588 ✪ The defeat of the Spanish Armada

1601 ✪ The Earl of Essex is executed

1603 ✪ Elizabeth dies at Richmond Palace. James I is king

First published in 2003 by the National Maritime Museum, Greenwich, London, SE10 9NF

ISBN 978-0-948065-46-0

© National Maritime Museum 2003

2 3 4 5 6 7 8 9

A CIP catalogue record for this book is available from the British Library.

Commissioned by Rachel Giles
Editorial assistance by Alicia Worrall
Designed by Rachel Hamdi/Holly Fulbrook
Cover design by Mike Spoor
Illustrations by Gwyneth Williamson and Mike Spoor

This book has been published to accompany the exhibition 'Elizabeth' held at the National Maritime Museum, Greenwich 1 May – 14 Sept 2003.

Picture acknowledgements: Images © Trustees of the National Maritime Museum and by kind permission of the following: p2 (top) Hever Castle Ltd, Royal Collection, p3 Historic Royal Palaces, pp4, 6, 22 (top) and 26 National Portrait Gallery, p4 (top) Chequers Estate, p10 The Board of Trustees of the Armouries, p10 Private Collection, pp11,12 (left) Ashmolean Museum, Oxford, pp13 (top), 15, 22, and 23 British Museum, p13 Welbeck Abbey, pp14, 28 Victoria & Albert Museum, p16 Honourable Society of the Middle Temple, p19 Ulster Museum, p20 (bottom) The Burghley House Collection, p27 (top) Public Records Office, p27 British Library, p27 (bottom) by kind permission of the Duke of Norfolk, Arundel Castle.

The following are NMM photographic references. Pictures may be ordered from the Picture Library, National Maritime Museum, Greenwich, London SE10 9NF (tel. 020 8312 6600). All © National Maritime Museum, London:

p2 BHC2763; p5 D2635; p9 D2687 and (bottom) BHC4190; p13 BHC2680; p15 (top) PU4362; p15 PU132; p17 E9304 and (top) E9047; p18 BHC2662 and (bottom) E0433; p20 E9271 and E9304; p24 BHC1262; p25 (top) E9048 and E3398; p28 BHC2796.

Printed in China.

Sponsored by Morgan Stanley

Elizabeth

Contents

My family

Greenwich Palace, 1533

'My parents, Henry VIII and Anne Boleyn, were very, very, disappointed that I wasn't a prince. All the jousts they'd planned to celebrate the birth of a son were cancelled!'

Elizabeth was not Henry's first child. He had a daughter, Mary, from his first marriage to Katherine of Aragon. Henry desperately wanted a son to succeed him. When Katherine became too old to have more children, he decided to divorce her.

Elizabeth's mother,
Anne Boleyn

You promised
me a prince!

Elizabeth's father,
Henry VIII

Henry asked the Pope, who was head of the Catholic church, to end his marriage to Katherine. The Pope refused, so Henry made himself the head of his own church and got the divorce he wanted.

Joust
Cancelled